MCR

FEB 1 7 2009

Team Spirit

THE LOS ANGELES CLIPPERS

BY

MARK STEWART

Content Consultant
Matt Zeysing
Historian and Archivist
The Naismith Memorial Basketball Hall of Fame

NORWOOD HOUSE 🏠 PRESS

CHICAGO, ILLINOIS

Norwood House Press
P.O. Box 316598
Chicago, Illinois 60631

For information regarding Norwood House Press, please visit our website at:
www.norwoodhousepress.com or call 866-565-2900.

All photos courtesy of Getty Images except the following:
Topps, Inc. (6, 7, 14, 20, 21, 22, 35 top left, 37, 38, 40 top & bottom left, 43),
The Star Co. (9, 34 right, 36), Century Publishing Co. (28), Panini (35 bottom right).
Cover: Noah Graham, NBAE/Getty Images
Special thanks to Topps, Inc.

Editor: Mike Kennedy
Designer: Ron Jaffe
Project Management: Black Book Partners, LLC.
Research: Joshua Zaffos

Special thanks to Bill Schultz

Library of Congress Cataloging-in-Publication Data

Stewart, Mark, 1960-
  The Los Angeles Clippers / by Mark Stewart ; content consultant,
Matt Zeysing.
    p. cm. -- (Team spirit)
  Includes bibliographical references and index.
  Summary: "Presents the history and accomplishments of the Los
Angeles Clippers basketball team. Includes highlights of players,
coaches and awards, quotes, timelines, maps, glossary and websites"
--Provided by publisher.
  ISBN-13: 978-1-59953-290-5 (library edition : alk. paper)
  ISBN-10: 1-59953-290-5 (library edition : alk. paper) 1. Los
Angeles Clippers (Basketball team)--History--Juvenile literature. I.
Zeysing, Matt.
II. Title.
  GV885.52.L65S74 2009
  796.323'640979494--dc22
                                                    2008038136

COVER PHOTO: The Clippers celebrate a win during the 2005–06 season.

Table of Contents

SPORTS WORDS & VOCABULARY WORDS: In this book, you will find many words that are new to you. You may also see familiar words used in new ways. The glossary on page 46 gives the meanings of basketball words, as well as "everyday" words that have special basketball meanings. These words appear in **bold type** throughout the book. The glossary on page 47 gives the meanings of vocabulary words that are not related to basketball. They appear in ***bold italic type*** throughout the book.

BASKETBALL SEASONS: Because each basketball season begins late in one year and ends early in the next, seasons are not named after years. Instead, they are written out as two years separated by a dash, for example 1944–45 or 2005–06.

Meet the Clippers

Some **professional** basketball teams seem to have all the luck. They find **_extraordinary_** players where no one else thinks to look. They make wild, buzzer-beating shots. They win games when they are not at their best. The Los Angeles Clippers could have used some of this luck over the years. Their search for a winning **_formula_** has taken them through a lot of good times, but some bad times, too.

Perhaps that is why Clippers fans are so **_devoted_** to their team. No club has played in the **National Basketball Association (NBA)** longer without reaching the **NBA Finals**. The Clippers remind us that life can be a struggle—but also that some things are worth it. That is why you never stop trying.

This book tells the story of the Clippers. They have had some great players over the years, and their fans believe the team will someday win it all. When that championship comes, it won't just be an amazing day for Los Angeles. It will be a special day for sports.

The Clippers huddle to discuss their game plan during the 2007–08 season.

Way Back When

The Clippers began their basketball journey 2,500 miles away from Los Angeles in Buffalo, New York. They joined the NBA as the Braves for the 1970–71 season. The team's first star was Bob Kauffman.

BOB McADOO • C

He was a **burly** forward with a smooth outside shot. The team's first coach was Dolph Schayes. He had been a star player for the Syracuse Nationals of the NBA. Like Buffalo, Syracuse is a city in western New York State.

During the early 1970s, the Braves added more good players, including Bob McAdoo and Randy Smith. McAdoo was an unstoppable scorer who played forward and center. Few big men have ever shot as well. Smith was one of the quickest guards in the NBA—and also one of the toughest. He set a league record by playing in 906 games in a row.

With McAdoo and Smith leading the way, the Braves made it to the **playoffs** three years in a row from 1973–74 to 1975–76. Unfortunately, the team always ran into an opponent with more experience. Buffalo won only one **postseason** series during that period.

In 1978, the owner of the Braves, John Y. Brown, traded teams with Irv Levin, the owner of the Boston Celtics. Brown had owned the Kentucky Colonels, one of the best teams in the old **American Basketball Association (ABA)**. He loved the idea of owning the mighty Celtics. Levin preferred to own a team in his home state of California, so he moved the Braves to the city of San Diego and renamed them the Clippers.

The Clippers won 43 games in 1978–79. Their top players included Randy Smith, World B. Free, Freeman Williams, and Swen Nater. Free finished second in the league in scoring. The following year, Bill Walton joined the Clippers. The fans in San Diego were very excited to have the star center. However, injuries kept him off the court for most of his time with the Clippers. For the next 10 seasons, the team struggled to win games.

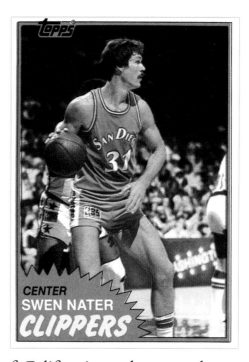

LEFT: Bob McAdoo, Buffalo's top star during the 1970s.
ABOVE: A trading card featuring Swen Nater, who became one of the Clippers' most popular players.

The Clippers moved north to Los Angeles for the 1984–85 season. Derek Smith, Norm Nixon, and Marques Johnson starred for the team over the next few years. However, the Clippers' luck did not improve until the 1990s, when they made it to the playoffs three times. The team had a number of good players during that time, including Ken Norman, Charles Smith, Danny Manning, Loy Vaught, Ron Harper, and Eric Piatkowski.

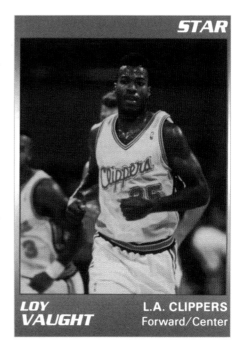

The person who helped build the Clippers into a consistent winner was Elgin Baylor. He had starred in the NBA for 14 seasons and was voted into the **Hall of Fame** in 1977. Baylor was hired by Los Angeles to run the club's business.

Toward the end of the 1990s, the Clippers decided to rebuild their team with a new group of players. It took three long years, but by 2001 Los Angeles had a combination of young stars and *experienced* **veterans**. Each victory was still a hard-fought battle, but the fans now looked toward the 21st *century* with hope and excitement.

LEFT: Danny Manning drives to the basket. He was the leader of the Clippers during their best years of the 1990s.
ABOVE: Loy Vaught, who teamed up with Manning to give Los Angeles a great one-two punch.

The Team Today

For several years, the Clippers built their team around forwards Elton Brand and Corey Maggette. They had been teammates at Duke University, and in no time they became NBA stars. The Clippers mixed in a combination of young players and old players, but did not become a winner until 2005–06. That year the club won 47 games.

The Clippers soon became one of the NBA's toughest home-court teams. Their record in Los Angeles from 2004–05 to 2006–07 was 79–44! Prior to the 2008–09 season, Brand and Maggette decided to leave the Clippers. The team replaced them with **All-Star** Baron Davis and Marcus Camby, the 2007 NBA **Defensive Player of the Year**.

These two experienced players joined veterans Chris Kaman and Ricky Davis, plus young stars Eric Gordon and Al Thornton. Clippers fans sensed the team had started building a new foundation for success in the years to come.

Marcus Camby and Baron Davis talk things over during a 2008–09 game.

Home Court

Before moving to California, the team played its home games in Buffalo Memorial Auditorium. The Braves shared the arena with the Buffalo Sabres hockey team. Fans nicknamed the building the "Aud."

When the team moved west, it made its next home in the San Diego Sports Arena. After six years there, the Clippers moved again, this time north to the Los Angeles Memorial Sports Arena. Today, it is best known for hosting the show *American Gladiators*.

In 1999, the Clippers moved into a new arena. They share this building with the NBA Lakers, the **Women's National Basketball Association (WNBA)** Sparks, and the Kings hockey team.

BY THE NUMBERS

- *There are 18,997 seats for basketball in the Clippers' arena.*
- *The arena is also used for political events, ice skating shows, and music concerts. Nearly 4,000,000 people visit the building each year.*
- *The arena is 950,000 square feet.*
- *The arena features an eight-sided scoreboard with four huge video screens.*

The Clippers are the home team against Kobe Bryant and the Los Angeles Lakers during a 2007–08 game.

Dressed for Success

The main colors of the Buffalo Braves started as black, white, and orange. The team *logo* included a feather from a Native American *headdress*. In 1973–74, the Braves switched their main color to light blue. When the team moved to California and became the Clippers, it changed its logo to show a clipper ship, which is a kind of sailboat.

The Clippers continued to use blue as a main color, but they experimented with the shade several times over the years. They used a dark blue after moving to Los Angeles in 1984. In the late 1980s, the Clippers switched to red as their main color. Since then, they have used different combinations of red, white, and blue.

The Clippers have also changed their logo over the years. The team switched to a basketball instead of a clipper, because sailing was a more popular sport in San Diego than in Los Angeles.

FORWARD

BRAVES

BOB KAUFFMAN

Bob Kauffman wears the original black, white, and orange uniform of the Braves.

UNIFORM BASICS

The basketball uniform is very simple. It consists of a roomy top and baggy shorts.

- The top hangs from the shoulders, with big "scoops" for the arms and neck. This style has not changed much over the years.

- Shorts, however, have changed a lot. They used to be very short, so players could move their legs freely. In the last 20 years, shorts have actually gotten longer and much baggier.

Basketball uniforms look the same as they did long ago … until you look very closely. In the old days, the shorts had belts and buckles. The tops were made of a thick cotton called "jersey," which got very heavy when players sweated. Later, uniforms were made of shiny *satin*. They may have looked great, but they did not "breathe." Players got very hot! Today, most uniforms are made of *synthetic* materials that soak up sweat and keep the body cool.

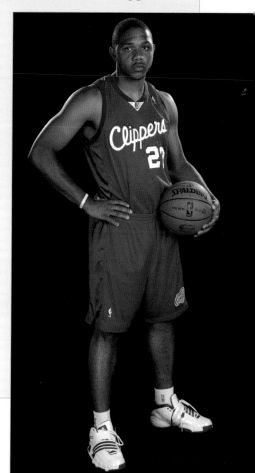

Eric Gordon models the Clippers' 2008–09 away uniform.

We Won!

Playoff wins have not come easily to the Clippers over the years. So the team's fans have learned to *savor* each one. The Clippers' first win came in 1974, when they were playing in Buffalo as the Braves. Bob McAdoo led the team into battle against the Boston

Celtics. The Braves lost the first game of the series before winning the first postseason contest in team history. Buffalo went down again in Game 3 and then tied the series with another victory. Unfortunately, Boston still triumphed. The Celtics went on to win the NBA Championship.

The Braves reached the playoffs again in the 1974–75 season. This time, they played the Washington Bullets. The series lasted seven games and featured an *unforgettable* duel between McAdoo and Elvin Hayes. McAdoo won the battle—he averaged 37.4 points and scored 50 in one game—but lost the war. The Bullets took Game 7 and, like the Celtics the year before,

ABOVE: Bob McAdoo rises for a jump shot during the 1975 playoffs against the Washington Bullets.   RIGHT: Elton Brand makes a move against the Denver Nuggets during the 2006 playoffs.

they made it all the way to the NBA Finals.

One year later, the Braves won a playoff series for the first time. They beat the Philadelphia 76ers in a best-of-three series. Each team won one game, which set up a winner-take-all Game 3 in Philadelphia. McAdoo was a one-man show. He scored 51 points and grabbed 22 rebounds. The Braves beat the 76ers 124–123 in **overtime**. Unfortunately, the Braves ran into the red-hot Celtics after that. They lost the series in six games. Once again, Boston went on to win the NBA Championship.

No one knew it then, but it would be 30 years before the Clippers tasted victory again in the playoffs. In the spring of 2006, Los Angeles won its first playoff series since moving to California. The team had talented players at every position. Elton Brand, Chris Kaman, and Corey Maggette made up the front line. Sam Cassell, Cuttino Mobley, and Shaun Livingston starred in the backcourt.

The Clippers faced off against the Denver Nuggets. They won Game 1 by a score of 89–87. Brand was the hero. He blocked a shot in the closing seconds to save the victory.

Brand, with help from Mobley, also led the Clippers to a win in Game 2. Denver came back to win Game 3, but the Clippers finished off the Nuggets in the next two games. Livingston was sensational in both victories. He had 14 **assists** in the last game of the series.

Playoff fever swept Los Angeles. But for a change, it was the Clippers making headlines. While the Clippers were winning their series, the Lakers had lost to the Phoenix Suns. California basketball fans were disappointed that the Lakers and Clippers would not

meet. But the Clippers provided plenty of thrills against Phoenix in the next round.

Although few experts gave the Clippers a chance, they won three games in the series—and almost took a fourth in double-overtime. The Suns barely survived their battle with the "other" team from Los Angeles. When the Phoenix players left the floor after Game 7, they had a new respect for the Clippers. So did everyone else in the NBA.

LEFT: Sam Cassell is all smiles after the Clippers' victory in Game 5 over the Nuggets.   **ABOVE**: Corey Maggette soars to the rim for a layup against the Phoenix Suns.

Go-To Guys

To be a true star in the NBA, you need more than a great shot. You have to be a "go-to guy"—someone teammates trust to make the winning play when the seconds are ticking away in a big game. Fans of the Braves and Clippers have had a lot to cheer about over the years, including these great stars …

THE PIONEERS

RANDY SMITH   6´ 3˝ Guard

• BORN: 12/12/1948   • PLAYED FOR TEAM: 1971–72 TO 1978–79

Randy Smith began his career as a forward. When the Braves moved him to guard, he became one of the best players in the NBA. Smith used his soft jump shot to average 20 points a game four years in a row during the 1970s.

BOB McADOO   6´ 9˝ Center/Forward

• BORN: 9/25/1951   • PLAYED FOR TEAM: 1972–73 TO 1976–77

Bob McAdoo might have been the best-shooting big man in basketball history. He had a quick release and a smooth touch. McAdoo led the NBA in scoring three times and was named the league's **Most Valuable Player (MVP)** in 1974–75.

ABOVE: Randy Smith   **RIGHT**: Jim McMillian

ERNIE DiGREGORIO   6´ 0˝ Guard

- BORN: 1/15/1951   • PLAYED FOR TEAM: 1973–74 TO 1976–77

Everyone knew Ernie DiGregorio as "Ernie D." He was one of the smartest passers in the league. When he and Randy Smith formed Buffalo's backcourt, the team was tough to beat. DiGregorio was also an excellent free-throw shooter.

JIM McMILLIAN   6´ 5˝ Forward

- BORN: 3/11/1948   • PLAYED FOR TEAM: 1973–74 TO 1975–76

Jim McMillian brought a winning attitude to the Braves. He had previously been a member of the NBA champion Los Angeles Lakers. In McMillian's three years in Buffalo, the team won 134 games.

BILL WALTON   6´ 11˝ Center

- BORN: 11/5/1952   • PLAYED FOR TEAM: 1979–80 TO 1984–85

Clippers fans still talk about what might have been had Bill Walton stayed healthy. Unfortunately, in six seasons with the team, he played only 169 games.

JIM McMILLIAN • F

When Walton was on the court for the Clippers, he was one of the most brilliant centers in history.

DANNY MANNING   6´ 10˝ Forward

- BORN: 5/17/1966   • PLAYED FOR TEAM: 1988–89 TO 1993–94

The Clippers made Danny Manning the first pick in the 1988 NBA **draft**. He hurt his knee as a **rookie**, but came back to be one of the league's best **all-around** players. Manning represented the Clippers in the **All-Star Game** twice.

LOY VAUGHT   6′ 9″ Forward

• BORN: 2/27/1968   • PLAYED FOR TEAM: 1990–91 TO 1997–98

During the 1990s, Loy Vaught was the team's most dependable player. He was a good scorer and rebounder—and an even tougher competitor and leader.

ELTON BRAND   6′ 8″ Forward

• BORN: 3/11/1979

• PLAYED FOR TEAM: 2001–02 TO 2007–08

The Clippers were never known for paying their players a lot of money—until Elton Brand came along. In 2003, the team signed him to an $82 million contract. Night in and night out, Brand scored 20 points and pulled down 10 rebounds, with plenty of blocks, assists, and steals.

COREY MAGGETTE   6′ 6″ Forward

• BORN: 11/12/1979

• PLAYED FOR TEAM: 2000–01 TO 2007–08

No one liked to guard Corey Maggette. He could make a monster dunk one time down the court, and then connect on a long **3-pointer** the next time down the court. Maggette averaged more than 20 points a game three times for the Clippers.

ABOVE: Elton Brand   **RIGHT**: Baron Davis

CHRIS KAMAN   7´ 0˝ Center

• BORN: 4/28/1982   • FIRST SEASON WITH TEAM: 2003–04

The Clippers picked Chris Kaman in the first round of the 2003 NBA draft. Fans liked him immediately for his hard work and tough defense. In 2007–08, Kaman led the team in rebounding and averaged nearly 16 points a game.

BARON DAVIS   6´ 3˝ Guard

• BORN: 4/13/1979

• FIRST SEASON WITH TEAM: 2008–09

Baron Davis made his reputation as a scorer, **playmaker**, and also a *movie producer*. When he joined the Clippers, it was a match made in Hollywood. Los Angeles got an All-Star leader, and Davis got to star in the movie capital of the world.

MARCUS CAMBY   6´ 11˝ Center/ Forward

• BORN: 3/22/1974

• FIRST SEASON WITH TEAM: 2008–09

Fans may love high scoring, but defense wins games in the NBA. That is why the Clippers signed Marcus Camby. He was the league's Defensive Player of the Year for the 2006–07 season.

On the Sidelines

The Clippers have had some excellent coaches over the years. During their days as the Buffalo Braves, they had great success under Jack Ramsay. He later coached the Portland Trailblazers to the 1977 NBA Championship.

In San Diego, the Clippers' coaches included Gene Shue and Paul Silas. Shue coached the Philadelphia 76ers against Ramsay in the 1977 NBA Finals and was named **Coach of the Year** twice. Silas had played in the NBA Finals as a member of the Boston Celtics and Seattle Supersonics.

In 1981, Donald Sterling bought the Clippers. After moving the team to Los Angeles, he continued to look for top coaches. Over the years, some of the NBA's best worked on the sidelines for the Clippers. Don Chaney, Larry Brown, Bill Fitch, and Mike Dunleavy all led the team at one time or another. Dunleavy coached Los Angeles to 47 victories in 2005–06 and later set a team record for victories in a career.

Donald Sterling and Elgin Baylor pose for a picture during the Clippers' great playoff run in 2006.

One Great Day

In the early 1990s, the Clippers had lots of talent on their **roster**. Among the best players was Charles Smith, a long-armed forward with a smooth turnaround jump shot. In a game against the Nuggets in Denver, Smith couldn't miss. The Clippers kept feeding him the ball near the basket, and he kept scoring.

Smith's personal best was 40 points. At the end of the third quarter, he had 41. The Nuggets tried everything and everyone against Smith—including his old college teammate Jerome Lane. Nothing worked. "I've never seen him play like that," Lane said afterwards.

The Clippers led the game from beginning to end and scored 11 points in the final two minutes to win 137–121. Smith finished with 52 points. That total tied Bob McAdoo for the team record. "If I'd known the club record, I'd have gone for it," Smith claimed. "I think I could have gotten another bucket if I had known what the record was."

Why did Smith and the Clippers have an advantage in their game against the Nuggets? They had watched Denver play the New

Charles Smith looks for an opening in the defense. He was unstoppable against the Denver Nuggets in December of 1990.

Jersey Nets the night before. Smith saw that the Nuggets were leaving his favorite spot open. "I figured out from that game what I thought would work," he said. "I told the guards to get me the ball, that I thought I could score."

Legend Has It

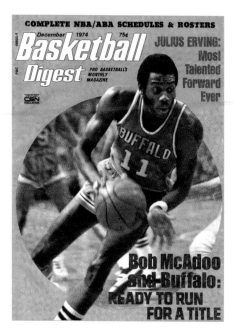

Who was the most forgetful player in the NBA?

LEGEND HAS IT that Bob McAdoo was. When NBA players travel from city to city, the team usually takes care of every detail. Planes, buses, hotels—everything is arranged in advance. All the players need to do is pack their bags. According to McAdoo's teammates, this was not his strong point. He always seemed to leave important items at home before road trips, and he often checked out of hotels with clothes still in the closets and drawers. McAdoo drove the team especially crazy when he would forget his basketball shoes in the hotel room. Garfield Heard summed his teammate up in an interview one day. "He's the worst packer in pro ball," said Heard.

ABOVE: A magazine cover of Bob McAdoo, Buffalo's most forgetful player.   **RIGHT**: "Bingo!" Ralph Lawler waves to the crowd during his 2,000th game as the Clippers' announcer.

Did the Clippers almost become Florida's first NBA team?

LEGEND HAS IT that they did. In 1976, a wealthy Florida couple named the Cowans agreed on a handshake to buy the Braves. They planned to move the club to the city of Hollywood, an hour north of Miami. Braves fans were furious, and the city of Buffalo tried to block the sale. The Cowans got nervous and walked away without buying the team.

Why do Clipper fans yell "Bingo" after 3-pointers?

LEGEND HAS IT that they are yelling the name of Bingo Smith. He was famous for his long-range shooting during the 1970s. Smith only played one season for the Clippers, but it was the first year the NBA used the 3-point shot. He launched 76 3-pointers for the team that

season and made 22 of them. The "Bingo" *tradition* was started by Ralph Lawler, the Clippers' broadcaster.

It Really Happened

When an NBA coach gives a speech in the locker room at halftime, he expects his players to listen. At halftime of a 2006 game against the New Orleans Hornets, Mike Dunleavy demanded that the Clippers play better defense. The Hornets had made more than half of their shots in the first two quarters and led 51–47.

The Clippers took the floor in the second half expecting to do better. Dunleavy was confident they would. Still, no one could believe what happened next. Try as they might, the Hornets could not score a basket. Good defense and bad luck added up to only 16 points in the final 24 minutes.

"I think it was our communication on defense," said Clippers guard Sam Cassell. "When we do that, we're at our best. When we don't communicate, we get our butts whipped. It's just that simple."

During one stretch, the Clippers outscored the Hornets 25–0. The 16 points by New Orleans were the fewest scored in a half since the NBA began using the 24-second shot clock in 1954.

ABOVE: Mike Dunleavy watches the action from the sideline.
RIGHT: After their coach's halftime speech, the Clippers didn't allow any easy baskets by the New Orleans Hornets.

Team Spirit

Clippers fans are among the most devoted in the NBA. Some people think of the "Clips" as the "other" team in Los Angeles, far behind the Lakers. But to Clippers fans, they are the "only" team.

"Clipper Nation" is a group of fans that get together at games and online. They take pictures of themselves all over the world wearing Clippers caps and shirts and send them in to the team's web site. Like Southern California, Clipper Nation is made up of people from all walks of life.

Something else fans of the Clippers have in common is their love for Ralph Lawler. He has broadcast almost every game since the team moved west from Buffalo. Millions of Californians have grown up listening to his voice on television and radio. When a Clipper makes an amazing play, Lawler says, "Oh-me-oh-my!"

For many years, Lawler worked with Bill Walton, who had played for the Clippers. Both announcers had a great sense of humor. Fans loved the way they joked with each other.

Actor Billy Crystal is one of many Hollywood stars who loyally supports the Clippers. Crystal has been in movies such as *Cars, Monsters, Inc.,* and *The Princess Bride.*

Timeline

The basketball season is played from October through June. That means each season takes place at the end of one year and the beginning of the next. In this timeline, the accomplishments of the Braves and Clippers are shown by season.

1970–71
The team joins the NBA as the Buffalo Braves.

1984–85
The Clippers move to Los Angeles.

1975–77
Bob McAdoo is named league MVP.

1978–79
The team moves to San Diego and becomes the Clippers.

1983–84
Bill Walton sets a team record with 10 blocked shots in a game.

World B. Free, a star for the team after its move to San Diego.

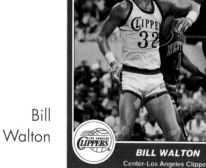

Bill Walton

STAR '85

BILL WALTON
Center-Los Angeles Clippers

Danny Manning

Marcus Camby

1988–89
The Clippers choose Danny Manning with the first pick in the draft.

2008–09
Baron Davis and Marcus Camby join the Clippers.

1990–91
Charles Smith ties the team record with 52 points in a game.

1998–99
The Clippers choose Michael Olowokandi with the first pick in the draft.

2003–04
Quentin Richardson makes eight 3-pointers in a game.

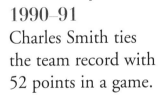

Charles Smith

Quentin Richardson

Fun Facts

MR. CLEAN

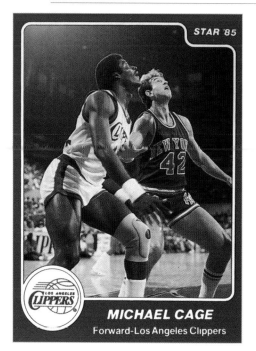

MICHAEL CAGE
Forward-Los Angeles Clippers

Michael Cage was the Clippers' best rebounder during the 1980s. His nickname was "Windex Man" because he "cleaned the glass" so well. Cage led the NBA in rebounds per game in 1987–88.

U'NIQUE

In 1994, the Clippers traded All-Star Danny Manning for All-Star Dominique Wilkins. "Nique" was incredible during his 25 games in a Clippers uniform. He averaged 29.1 points per game—the most ever for a forward in the history of the team.

STAR OF STARS

In 1978, Randy Smith was sent into the All-Star Game as a **substitute**. He scored 27 points, grabbed seven rebounds, and was named MVP of the game.

DREAMING BIG

In the early 1980s, one of the Clippers' best players was Joe Bryant. His young son told his dad's Clippers teammates that one day he too would play in the NBA. The young man kept his word. His name is Kobe Bryant.

DOING IT ALL

In 1973–74, Bob McAdoo averaged more than 30 points and 15 rebounds a game. No NBA player has matched those numbers for one season since.

WIN #1

The first game in team history was a 107–92 victory over the Cleveland Cavaliers. It was also the first game ever for the Cavaliers.

ON THE REBOUND

One of the most popular Clippers was Swen Nater. The 6'11" center led the NBA in rebounding in 1979–80. He set a team record with 32 rebounds in a game that season.

LEFT: Michael Cage, the Clippers' "Windex Man."
ABOVE: Joe Bryant, who played in the NBA before his son Kobe.

Talking Hoops

"Being a seventh-round **draft choice**, it was a brilliant opportunity to show everyone that I belonged in the NBA."
— *Randy Smith, on winning the MVP award in the 1978 All-Star Game*

Bill Walton
CENTER
CLIPPERS

"It was the biggest disappointment, biggest frustration in my life. In my hometown and everything! That was ***embarrassing***. You don't like to be a failure, and I was one."
— *Bill Walton, on the injuries that kept him out of more than 300 games with the Clippers*

"Basketball's always been my first love. I think I'm a good judge of talent. That's why I'm here."
— *Elgin Baylor, on his 20-plus years with the Clippers*

"I used to keep saying to myself, 'I'm not a center, I'm a **power forward**.' But eventually I gave up on that idea."
— *Michael Cage, on the move that made him the NBA rebounding champion*

"You work hard and stick with it, good things will happen. That's what I'm a believer of."

> —*Elton Brand, on leading the Clippers back to the playoffs*

"We loved the fans in L.A. They gave us so much over the years."

> —*Corey Maggette, on the loyalty of Clippers fans*

"To come home, and to be in the place where your dream first started—fifteen minutes away from where my grandfather built my first basketball court—is a dream come true."

> —*Baron Davis, on joining the Clippers in his hometown of Los Angeles*

LEFT: Bill Walton
RIGHT: Baron Davis

For the Record

The great Braves and Clippers teams and players have left their marks on the record books. These are the "best of the best" …

ERNIE DiGREGORIO · G

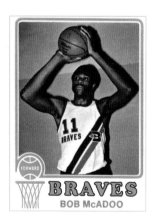

BRAVES
BOB McADOO

CLIPPERS AWARD WINNERS

WINNER	AWARD	SEASON
Bob McAdoo	Rookie of the Year*	1972–73
Ernie DiGregorio	Rookie of the Year	1973–74
Bob McAdoo	Most Valuable Player	1974–75
Adrian Dantley	Rookie of the Year	1976–77
Randy Smith	All-Star Game MVP	1977–78
Terry Cummings	Rookie of the Year	1982–83
Brent Barry	Slam Dunk Champion	1995–96
Bobby Simmons	Most Improved Player of the Year	2004–05

The Rookie of the Year award is given to the league's best first-year player.

TOP LEFT: Ernie DiGregorio
BOTTOM LEFT: Bob McAdoo
RIGHT: Bobby Simmons
FAR RIGHT: Brent Barry in action during the 1996 Slam Dunk Contest.

Pinpoints

The history of a basketball team is made up of many smaller stories. These stories take place all over the map—not just in the city a team calls "home." Match the push-pins on these maps to the Team Facts and you will begin to see the story of the Clippers unfold!

TEAM FACTS

1 Los Angeles, California—*The Clippers have played here since 1984–85.*

2 Buffalo, New York—*The team played here as the Braves from 1970–71 to 1977–78.*

3 San Diego, California—*The Clippers moved here in 1978–79.*

4 Hattiesburg, Mississippi—*Danny Manning was born here.*

5 Macon, Georgia—*Norm Nixon was born here.*

6 West Memphis, Arkansas—*Michael Cage was born here.*

7 Melrose Park, Illinois—*Corey Maggette was born here.*

8 Grand Rapids, Michigan—*Loy Vaught was born here.*

9 Brooklyn, New York—*Mike Dunleavy was born here.*

10 Philadelphia, Pennsylvania—*Jack Ramsay was born here.*

11 Greensboro, North Carolina—*Bob McAdoo was born here.*

12 Paris, France—*Dominique Wilkins was born here.*

Danny Manning

43

Play Ball

Basketball is a sport played by two teams of five players. NBA games have four 12-minute quarters—48 minutes in all—and the team that scores the most points when time has run out is the winner. Most baskets count for two points. Players who make shots from beyond the three-point line receive an extra point. Baskets made from the free-throw line count for one point. Free throws are penalty shots awarded to a team, usually after an opponent has committed a foul. A foul is called when one player makes hard contact with another.

Players can move around all they want, but the player with the ball cannot. He must bounce the ball with one hand or the other (but never both) in order to go from one part of the court to another. As long as he keeps "dribbling," he can keep moving.

In the NBA, teams must attempt a shot every 24 seconds, so there is little time to waste. The job of the defense is to make it as difficult as possible to take a good shot—and to grab the ball if the other team shoots and misses.

This may sound simple, but anyone who has played the game knows that basketball can be very complicated. Every player on the court has a job to do. Different players have different strengths and weaknesses. The coach must mix these players in just the right way, and teach them to work together as one.

The more you play and watch basketball, the more "little things" you are likely to notice. The next time you are at a game, look for these plays:

PLAY LIST

ALLEY-OOP—A play where the passer throws the ball just to the side of the rim—so a teammate can catch it and dunk in one motion.

BACK-DOOR PLAY—A play where the passer waits for his teammate to fake the defender away from the basket—then throws him the ball when he cuts back toward the basket.

KICK-OUT—A play where the ball-handler waits for the defense to surround him—then quickly passes to a teammate who is open for an outside shot. The ball is not really kicked in this play; the term comes from the action of pinball machines.

NO-LOOK PASS—A play where the passer fools a defender (with his eyes) into covering one teammate—then suddenly passes to another without looking.

PICK-AND-ROLL—A play where one teammate blocks or "picks off" another's defender with his body—then cuts to the basket for a pass in the confusion.

Glossary

BASKETBALL WORDS TO KNOW

3-POINTER—A basket made from behind the 3-point line.

ALL-AROUND—Good at all parts of the game.

ALL-STAR—A player selected to play in the annual All-Star Game.

ALL-STAR GAME—The annual game in which the best players from the East and the West play against each other. The game does not count in the standings.

AMERICAN BASKETBALL ASSOCIATION (ABA)—The basketball league that played for nine seasons starting in 1967. Prior to the 1976–77 season, four ABA teams joined the NBA, and the rest went out of business.

ASSISTS—Passes that lead to successful shots.

COACH OF THE YEAR—The award given each season to the league's best coach.

DEFENSIVE PLAYER OF THE YEAR—The award given each year to the league's best defensive player.

DRAFT—The annual meeting during which NBA teams choose from a group of the best college players. The draft is held each summer.

DRAFT CHOICE—A college player selected or "drafted" by NBA teams each summer.

HALL OF FAME—The museum in Springfield, Massachusetts, where basketball's greatest players are honored. A player voted into the Hall of Fame is sometimes called a "Hall of Famer."

MOST VALUABLE PLAYER (MVP)—The award given each year to the league's best player; also given to the best player in the league finals and All-Star Game.

NATIONAL BASKETBALL ASSOCIATION (NBA)—The professional league that has been operating since 1946–47.

NBA FINALS—The playoff series that decides the champion of the league.

OVERTIME—The extra period played when a game is tied after 48 minutes.

PLAYMAKER—Someone who helps his teammates score by passing the ball.

PLAYOFFS—The games played after the season to determine the league champion.

POSTSEASON—Another term for playoffs.

POWER FORWARD—The bigger and stronger of a team's two forwards.

PROFESSIONAL—A player or team that plays a sport for money.

ROOKIE—A player in his first season.

ROSTER—The list of players on a team.

SUBSTITUTE—A player who begins most games on the bench.

VETERANS—Players with great experience.

WOMEN'S NATIONAL BASKETBALL ASSOCIATION (WNBA)—The professional league for women that started in 1996.

OTHER WORDS TO KNOW

BURLY—Having a large, strong body.

CENTURY—A period of 100 years.

DEVOTED—Loyal.

EMBARRASSING—A feeling of dismay.

EXPERIENCED—Having knowledge and skill in a job.

EXTRAORDINARY—Unusual, or unusually talented.

FORMULA—A set way of doing something.

HEADDRESS—A fancy covering for the head.

LOGO—A symbol or design that represents a company or team.

MOVIE PRODUCER—The person responsible for the business areas of making a movie.

SATIN—A smooth, shiny fabric.

SAVOR—Enjoy fully and completely.

SYNTHETIC—Made in a laboratory, not in nature.

TRADITION—A belief or custom that is handed down from generation to generation.

UNFORGETTABLE—Amazing.

Places to Go

ON THE ROAD

LOS ANGELES CLIPPERS
1111 S. Figueroa Street
Los Angeles, California 90015
(213) 742-7250

NAISMITH MEMORIAL BASKETBALL HALL OF FAME
1000 West Columbus Avenue
Springfield, Massachusetts 01105
(877) 4HOOPLA

ON THE WEB

THE NATIONAL BASKETBALL ASSOCIATION   www.nba.com
  • *Learn more about the league's teams, players, and history*

THE LOS ANGELES CLIPPERS   www.nba.com/clippers
  • *Learn more about the Clippers*

THE BASKETBALL HALL OF FAME   www.hoophall.com
  • *Learn more about history's greatest players*

ON THE BOOKSHELF

To learn more about the sport of basketball, look for these books at your library or bookstore:

  • Hareas, John. *Basketball*. New York, New York: DK, 2005.

  • Hughes, Morgan. *Basketball*. Vero Beach, Florida: Rourke Publishing, 2005.

  • Thomas, Keltie. *How Basketball Works*. Berkeley, California: Maple Tree Press, distributed through Publishers Group West, 2005.

Index

PAGE NUMBERS IN **BOLD** REFER TO ILLUSTRATIONS.

The Team

MARK STEWART has written more than 20 books on basketball, and over 100 sports books for kids. He grew up in New York City during the 1960s rooting for the Knicks and Nets, and now takes his two daughters, Mariah and Rachel, to watch them play. Mark comes from a family of writers. His grandfather was Sunday Editor of *The New York Times* and his mother was Articles Editor of *The Ladies Home Journal* and *McCall's*. Mark has profiled hundreds of athletes over the last 20 years. He has also written several books about his native New York, and New Jersey, his home today. Mark is a graduate of Duke University, with a degree in history. He lives with his daughters and wife, Sarah, overlooking Sandy Hook, New Jersey.

MATT ZEYSING is the resident historian at the Basketball Hall of Fame in Springfield, Massachusetts. His research interests include the origins of the game of basketball, the development of professional basketball in the first half of the twentieth century, and the culture and meaning of basketball in American society.